Frantastically Frances

Thanks Marilyn
Frances North

The Sayings and Snarks
of My Mama, the Senior

Marilyn,
Thanks! Best wishes!
Sharon Rae North

by Sharon Rae North
illustrations by Alvin Maurice Long

Published by: Sharon Rae North
www.SharonRaeNorth.com
info@SharonRaeNorth.com

Copyright ©2022 Sharon Rae North
Copyright ©2022 illustrations Alvin M. Long

ISBN paperback book: 978-0-578-36058-4
ISBN e-book: 978-0-578-39736-8

Library of Congress Control Number: 2022901283

First Edition
First Printing, 2022

Printed in the United States of America

Be advised, this is not a children's book. It contains profanity and there may be words and conversation topics some may find offensive.

ACKNOWLEDGEMENTS

First, thanks to God for giving me the fortitude to see this project through to fruition.

Thanks to Mom for giving me enough anecdotes to actually write a book. I know your life story could fill many more pages (it would make a great novel). Even more so, thanks for being Gin's and my mother. We wouldn't be here without you (literally). Seriously though, thank you for all the sacrifices you made for us, standing in the gap as a single parent. Thanks for loving us unconditionally. Thanks for never giving up on us or letting us fall through the cracks. Thanks for being the kind of mother every child deserves, even when we didn't realize it. We are who we are, because of you and we love you with all our heart.

Thanks to Ginger for being the best big sister ever, hands down. Thanks to my brother-in-love, Luther, my niece Leisha and my nephew Luther Jr. and my niece-in-love, Casey for being my family (not that you had any choice in the matter).

Love you guys!

FORWARD

Some people may think of our mother, Frances North, as stern and no nonsense, but my sister Ginger and I have always known while that may be somewhat valid, she's also absolutely hilarious. Ginger calls it "Francesisms."

Now, legions of other people know it too. Several years ago, I started randomly posting on Facebook some of the things she says. The comments I received were often really funny. When I didn't post about her for a while people would send me direct messages, asking if she'd said anything funny or what comment she may have made about a television program, or a new hairstyle I was trying. She had a following without even having a FB account.

Some of her 'fans' suggested we develop a sitcom, or a blog or…a book. I was already ahead of them about the book.

I decided to revisit some FB posts I had made about her (no easy task given the number of years I've been posting), as well as just harvesting things she says day-to-day. That effort became *Frantastically Frances: The Sayings and Snarks of My Mama, the Senior*.

First, let me tell you a little about Mom. Born Frances Ivery in 1938, she was the youngest of the 14 Ivery children. Her eldest seven siblings were born in Georgia to Robert, a Methodist minister who worked in a steel mill, and Lillie, a Fire Baptized Holiness housewife and mother. The last seven were born in Youngstown, Ohio. There were 11 girls and three boys. My grandmother died when Mom was just 6 years old. She and the siblings closest to her in age were often shuffled around. Sometimes they lived with their grown sisters, but even spent time in foster care, with a lady named Campfire Brown. Due to his work schedule, their dad did not have adequate time to raise them, though he spent a lot of time with them. He died when Mom was 17, just a few months after she graduated high school. By the time she was 62 years old all her siblings were dead. All she had left were Ginger and her husband, Luther, her grandchildren, Luther Jr. and Leisha and me.

Mom raised Gin and me pretty much alone, having been divorced twice. She was sometimes strict and took no prisoners. But, as Gin and I look back, we understand. She was not going to let her children run her household or run over her. As we became adolescents, then smart-mouth teenagers, and snarky in our own right, Mom wasn't having it. She'd walk right up in our face and say, "You wanna hit me, don't you? I dare you." The way she said it and the look on her face removed any delusional thoughts we may have been having about trying to take her down. She would have killed us. As a matter of fact, she told us she would, "I will kill the shit in your behind," was one of her favorites, along with "I'll beat your ass 'til your nose bleeds." We turned out okay.

In 2003 Mom retired after working 32 years with Mahoning County in Youngstown. To Gin's and my surprise, she moved out of the house she'd lived in for more than 40 years and came to live with me, providing many years of material filling the pages of this book.

So, as you can see, the Francesisms have been a part of our lives for as long as we can remember. Now I'm sharing them with you.

Shhh. Don't let Mom know about this. She's already floated the idea of suing me for posting some of her comments on Facebook...LOL!

This book is dedicated to our Mom,
Frances W. North.

Thanks so much for all you've done and
continue to do, and just as much for all you
didn't do…but could have.

Thanks for loving us and for never feeling as
if your parental
responsibilities
ended just
because we
grew up.

Frantastically Frances

~ Unfiltered Francesisms ~

—•—

Ma: Jane Fonda is only a month older than me. She just got arrested for the 5th time. She's got me beat. I was only arrested three times.

Me: *--side eye—*

—•—

Ma: He's such a wisp…waps…whatever it's called.

Me: Wuss. It's called a wuss, Ma.

—•—

Ma filling out the DMV form:

Ma: It's got male, female, and non-binary. What is non-binary?

Me: Not you.

—•—

A Jeopardy question was about the store H&M. Ma said she didn't know what the H stood for. Plus, she said she thought it was about sex:

Me: That's S&M.

Ma: Well, that's what I've heard of…S&M.

———

Ma: I never undressed in front of my husband. In my day you just didn't do that. You didn't take off your clothes in front of a man.

Me: Well, you took off something. You have two kids.

Ma: *--100-yard stare glaring directly at me—*

———

Ma: You know we're 'bout to be snowed in and you just ate the last two Oreos. What kinda shit is that?

———

Ma sees the Vanity Fair cover with Kaitlyn Jenner on television:

Ma: Oh, she is pretty. Where'd she get the titties?

———

— · —

Ma waxing nostalgic during a conversation with Gin and me:

Ma: We rented a room at Tex and Mutt's down on Star Street.

Gin: You and Daddy...and y'all took a shower?

Me: Together?

Ma: We was screwing.

— · — · —

I was a Negro for a long time 'til they started calling us Black. And that was James Brown's fault. He made that song Say it Loud I'm Black and I'm Proud. When I was young if you called somebody Black, they beat your ass.

— · — · —

Ma: Wouldn't you think when somebody is ugly they would try to have a baby with somebody who looks better than them?

Me: Well, Ma, most people probably don't think they're ugly.

Ma: You know good and damn well somebody who's ugly knows they're ugly.

Me: You think so?

Ma: Yeah, and right now that boy is probably mad as hell at his mama.

—

Ma: These country girls...singing Dolly Parton and Johnny Gill.

Me: Vince Gil, Ma, not Johnny Gill.

Ma: Ain't there somebody named Johnny Gill?

Me: Yeah, he sings with New Edition.

Ma: Well, that's the one I've heard of.

—

Ma: You know them Republicans voted against that gun thing. What's wrong with them fuckers.

—

Ma: That's selfish of them. They ought to just put him to sleep.

Me: He's a man, Ma, not a dog. They don't just put people to sleep.

Ma: They don't? Guess that's why they put Dr. Kevorkian in jail

———

We moved into my newly built, beautiful townhouse and I hear Ma on the phone talking to my cousin:

Ma: …so, now that we live in the projects…

Me: WHAT???

Me talking to Ginger: Ma just called this the projects.

Ginger: No, she didn't.

Me: Yes, she did.

Ginger: I've never seen projects with granite countertops, wood floors.

Me: Fenced in back yard, two-car garage, and a master suite.

Ginger: Well, you know Ma.

———

Ma: I don't know if he's sterilizing anything. I ain't never seen any sterilizing equipment in his office."

Me *(perplexed):* Didn't he just do a procedure on your foot last week?

Ma: Peripheral artery disease... I thought they cut off your dad's legs because he had gonorrhea.

Me: Gonorrhea?

Ma: I meant gangrene.

Post-op and under anesthesia:

Nurse: Frances, I can't find your tissues.

Ma: My sister Wilma took them. She's a kleptomaniac.

Ginger and I were teasing Ma about how big her butt has gotten:

Ma: Yeah, now that I'm old and ain't nobody lookin' at it.

I might be a half fool,
but I ain't gonna be no whole one.

So, Ma and I ran into a few women today who had EXTREMELY bad breath. Ma later says to me:

Ma: Ain't never seen so many people in one day with breath smellin' like that. These girls better be careful havin' that oral sex. Mess around and end up with some STD in their throat. That's what happened to Little Murph...and he died.

--NO, I didn't even ask who Little Murph was--

So... I took Ma to the eye doctor. On the way home I was telling her about an article I was reading in a magazine in the lobby:

Ma: Why didn't you bring it with you?

Me: I couldn't just steal the people's magazine.

Ma: That ain't stealing. You just walk on out with it.

Then there was that time Mom, Gin and I toured the White House. We were barely in line outside when the Secret Service swooped down and got Ma. Nothing nefarious. They saw her using a walker and knew she'd need to go in a different way to avoid the stairs. Still, never a dull moment.

---

*Well, Ma got mad and yelled at me because I didn't
tell her I was washing a bunch of her baseball caps:*

Ma: Some of them hadn't even been worn, like
the one from PUNTA KINTE.

Me (laughing so hard I can't breathe, or even
talk): It's Punta Cana, Ma.

———

Ma: What's for dinner?

Me: Panko-parmesan cod and spinach salad

Ma: You know I don't eat spinach. Wouldn't even
feed it to y'all when you were kids. And I ain't never
heard of no panko.

Me: Here, just taste it.

Ma (chewing and frowing): You night wanna
turn that oven back on so I can put me a t.v. dinner
in it.

———

Ma: Steve Harvey looks like he should be
Pentecostal, but not with all that cussin' he does.

———

What goes against the Bible
goes against the Bible.
I don't think God changed His mind.

Ma: Kerry Washington is pretty, but she looks like when somebody kisses her, her teeth ought to bite 'em.

Mom and I were watching CBS Sunday Morning. Hillary Clinton was talking about the unrest in Egypt:

Me: Hillary is one smart woman.

Ma: That's why her head is so big...look at it.

Following a bad reaction to a medication that caused her tongue to swell:

Ma (sticking out her tongue): I'm the old Miley Cyrus.

Ma: Paul McCartney looks like somebody who'd scare you at night.

I said some folks are really cute babies, but then they grow up and are not attractive:

Ma: Anybody that's an ugly adult was an ugly baby.

———

Ma: That big fat one. What's his name?

Me: Chris Christie.

Ma: Yeah.

———

Me: If that's Pence's family, they're not very dressed up.

Ma: They got on Indiana clothes.

———

Ma just said I "uploaded" pictures into a photo album.

———

Me: It's called a circumcision, Ma, not "penis clipped."

———

Ma: I gotta learn how to use this Twiddle.

Me: Kindle, Ma. Kindle.

———

Ma, Ginger and I went to eat one Saturday:

Ma: This Chick-fil-A Icedream makes you dream you had some real ice cream.

———

Ma: I'm gonna have to take the rest of this food home.

Ginger: Ma, don't take that one chicken nugget and a French fry to Richmond.

———

Ma: That Denzel is a great actor. Remember how he came out that hotel room in *Flight* and was walking down the hall... with all that SWAGGER.

———

Ma: I put your fish in the oven to heat it up and forgot about it.

Me: You burned it?

Ma: Like a rock...maybe you can still eat it.

Me: *--crickets --*

———

Okay, why is Ma saying Oka Lonki instead of Manti T'eo?

———

Ma: I'm like this now 'cause I'm old and my memory is getting bad. I used to remember everything and was the smartest person on the planet.

———

Ma: Jack Nicholson always looks kinda raggedy and disheveled.

———

Ma and I were watching a movie with Isaac Hayes. I stepped away to do something and had my back to the TV when I heard shots:

Me: Ma, did he kill that woman?

Ma: Killed the shit out of her.

———

Me: And then she was showing pictures of dildos.

Ma: What's a dildo?

Me: Huh? You've never heard of a dildo?

Ma: I ain't never heard of a dildo. What is that?

Me: Look, I'll just show you the pictures.

———

Romance without finance is a nuisance.

My poor Mama opens a kitchen cabinet, and a can of soup falls out and bashes her in the forehead. Now she's sporting a lump and a big bruise over her right eye and has been holding a cold compress on it all evening. We laughed about it later…kinda.

Watching The Haves and the Have Nots:

Ma: What's 'fienen'?

--followed by--

Ma: Did she say 'bitchness?"

People want you to do well, just not better than them.

Folks saying religious dietary restrictions should exempt them from taking the COVID vaccine:

Ma: Always gonna be some maniac come up with some bullshit.

Ma: What did Alicia Keys name her baby?

Me: Egypt.

Ma: Ain't her husband Swizz Beatz?

Me: Yeah.

Ma: So the baby's name is Egypt Beatz?

Me: --LOL-- That's not his real last name.

Ma: Oh. Wonder what his nickname is, 'E' or maybe 'Gypt'?

Me: Don't know...maybe they just call him Egypt.

Ma: He's gonna hate them for that when he gets older.

———

Ma: She cooks 'bout as good as anybody else. It just tastes worse.

———

Long story short Ma is getting a tad forgetful, mixing up ovulation and orgasm:

Ma: It's been so long since I've had either one I can't remember which is which.

———

Follow a crazy kid home and you'll find crazy parents. Same with ugly.

—•—

So, Ma and I are watching 60 Minutes. Segment is about old people and how they've managed to live into their 80s and 90s. The question came up about sex:

Ma: Who would want to have sex at that age?

Me: What's wrong with that?

Ma: Because you're all dried up by then. I guess you can use some Vaseline or that gel. Then, a man that age probably can't even get it up.

Me: *--crickets—*

—•—

Me: Why ya up so early Ma?

Ma: I woke up.

—•—

Ma: Is that a real bear?

Me: A real teddy bear.

Ma: Then how is it walking and talking.

Me: Would a real bear be TALKING?

—•—

Here we go. So, Ma jumps all on me for using one of her gel writer pens. First of all, for the longest I gave you some of MY gel writers. You'd never even heard of gel writers. Then I started buying you your own when I'd stock up, so you could stop using mine. But, the convo went like this:

Ma: I had two pens on this table. Now, one is empty and the other one is gone.

Me: Oh, I had to write something down and mine are upstairs. I put it over there, let me get it.

Ma: You need to put my stuff back where you get it, or get your own.

———

Me: Ma, I'm not sure how you're using the words ventilator and vibrator interchangeably.

———

Ma is on the phone ordering checkbooks:

Me: Why do you order checks from the bank?

--she pauses--

Ma: I remember why I don't have to pay for them, because I'm a valuable customer... at least that's what he said.

———

Watching "Trail of Hope" with Ma:

Ma: White people die, it's a tragedy. Black people die, it's supposed to happen. Hmmm

---

Conversation about Steve Harvey:

Ma: If his lips wasn't so juicy, he wouldn't look like his breath stinks...he's got nice white teeth.

Ma: Them big girls always be kinda cute in the face.

So, she pulls the collar of her sweatshirt, tips her face/nose down toward her chest:

Ma: Every so often I seem to stink...I wash up daily, but I just don't seem to smell right...you know how old people smell.

Me: Ma you don't stink... trust me, I'd be the first to tell you if you got all funky.

Me: Ma, each time I've built a house you buy the custom shutters/blinds, washer and dryer.

Ma: You bought the house.

———

Ma: I want cornbread.

Me: Okay, I'll make you some. I'm gonna eat biscuits.

--*hour later*--

Ma: Those biscuits look good. I could've just ate those.

———

Ma and I were watching the news and talking about the 'drama' at Bobbi Kristina Brown's funeral:

Ma: You can take the fool out of the country, but you can't...uh, uh. You can take the country out of the boy, but you can't take the uh, uh.

Me: -- *trying REALLY hard not to laugh so my stomach won't hurt, 10 days post-op major surgery--*

Ma: You can take the boy out of the country, but you can't take the fool out of the fool.

Me: -- *doubled over laughing, and in pain--*

Ma: Well, you can't take the fool out of the fool.

———

You can't make no false promises to God.

Did my Mama just say something about police having Glocks?

Ma: I like every kind of music...except rap. The only rap I like is Ice T, LL Cool J and Snoop Dogg. And I really like Snoop Dogg a lot. I used to like Queen Latifah, but then she started singing regular songs.

Mom and I are in the car and Sirius XM Fly is on:

Ma: That sounds like Snoop Dogg.

Me: It is.

Ma: Then why does the screen say Dr. Dre?

Me: They did this song together.

Ma *GASP*: Did he just say "Ain't no pussy good enough to get burned while I'm up in it?"

Me: Uh oh, yeah. Lemme turn on Watercolors.

The Foo Fighters are performing on TV:

Ma: Hurry up and stop. Ohhh Myyyy Gawwwwd.

And again, Ma and I are in my car. Since I've been in the car several times today I know, unlike last time when I had on Sirius XM Fly, it's set to the Prince tribute channel. Turn on the radio and immediately:

Prince: "You sexy mother fucker."

MA *GASP*:

Me: Lemme turn on Watercolors.

I'm in the family room... had been watching a show for about 90 minutes:

Ma: Let's see if we're missing something good."

--Picks up the remote and changes the channel. (in my head ... Really, Ma?)--

---

I noticed some dust on the headboard of Ma's bed:

Me: I'm gonna have to dust your headboard.

Ma: I'm dusting it now.

--Wiping her bare hands over the surface--

Ma: When Andrea Bocelli sings people start crying.

Me: Yeah.

Ma: His voice is beautiful...but, I've never seen him with his eyes open.

Me: Maybe they don't open.

Ma: I've seen blind people with their eyes open. But I guess if you can't see what would be the point of them opening.

Ma: I should sleep in my clothes, then I won't have to put them on tomorrow.

Me: You ain't gonna wash up?

Ma: It takes me so long. I'm getting slower and slower.

You know what got me the most this year...when they wouldn't let me get a new driver's license just because I couldn't read those letters.

I'd recently had eye surgery and Ma wanted to go Christmas shopping:

Ma: You and me out here in this mall is the blind leading the blind.

———

Ma: Shawty?

Me: Urban for shorty.

Ma: Mmmmm

———

So, I just explained to Ma how beepers and pagers worked and what it meant when folks used to say, "Hit me on the hip."

———

There was a story on the news about the federal trial of the former Virginia governor. They went over some of the testimony from a former 'friend' of the governor and his wife:

Ma: Bet he was sleeping with both of them, having a TWAGE-MA-HAL.

Me: A what? I think you mean ménage a trois.

Ma: I knew that was wrong. I just couldn't remember what it was called.

———

Watching Jeopardy Mom and I were discussing the Constitution, Declaration of Independence, and the Gettysburg Address. We were trying to remember how the Declaration began, then the preamble to the Constitution. We kept mixing them up until finally:

Ma: "Why did they need all that shit. No wonder the country is all messed up."

--I still haven't figured out how she thought Benjamin Franklin had been president--

They came up with all kinda shit, and call it music.

Ma: What is he saying?

Me: Forrest Gump.

Ma: A song called Forrest Gump?

Me: Yeah .

Ma: He shoulda picked something else...I would feel bad if I'd paid money to get in there and heard this shit.

Kelly Clarkson singing Natural Woman:

Ma: You need to leave that one to the Black folks, baby. She didn't kill that one.

Okay, I'm SHOCKED. All of a sudden, my mother just sang, "We coulda had it alllll, rollin' in the deeeeep." I had no idea she even knew about that song, let alone knew some of the words.

Ma: There's a Jimmy Kimmel and a Jimmy Leno.

Me: Fallon

Ma: What did I say?

Me: Jimmy Leno

Ma: Oh. *--bursts out laughing—*

My mother just said Academy Award winning actor Forest Whitaker looks like a Black Shrek.

I had Ma at the office with me one day. I introduced her to a co-worker she hadn't met before. She asks him if he is Indian. He told her he is from India.

She then proceeds to tell him she likes Indian doctors because two of them saved her life when she had cancer. She said they were able to save her because they have "small hands." Fortunately, he continued speaking to me.

———

I had on a really cute dress:
Ma: Aren't you glad you're pretty.
Me: Lots of people say I look like you, Mom.

———

Ma on American Idol Contestant:
Ma: He's got a wang to his voice.
Me: I think you mean twang, Ma.
Ma: It used to be wang.
Me: I don't think so, Ma. It was never wang.

———

Ma: They don't make songs like this anymore. Everything is rap and cussin'.

———

Everybody's money

don't spend.

Every night I give Ma a kiss before I go to bed:

Me: Goodnight. You're my favorite Mommy.

Ma: Night. You're one of my favorite daughters.

--Well dang, she only has two. Whassup, Ma?--

———

Vic: You're gaining weight. You probably need to exercise more.

Ma: So are you. Look at your stomach.

Vic: That's my shirt.

Ma: I ain't never seen a fat shirt.

———

Ma: The first ladies always have to have some kinda mess. Michelle Obama 'done' started those gardens and changing the school menu...trying to take the fat off the kids.

———

Ma: What is that she has on? Oh, you know I'm blind. That's the stand.

--How she can mistake a lectern for an outfit... your guess is as good as mine--

———

Ma: Look at these fools at IHOP; just standin' in line...for some pancakes.

Me: Ma, why are you diggin' in your nose.

Ma: 'Cause it's mine and I can dig in it. It ain't like I'm diggin' in yours...(pause)...though I used to when you were little. Kids have boogers.

So, my greens are done and ready to go to the office party. They've cooked down a lot, as greens do:

Ma: That's enough. You can't feed the world. Now put some in a bowl for me so I can eat 'em tomorrow.

Ma is giving this poor nurse holy hell. He told her to NOT take her own insulin again while she' s here because she has to take theirs. The battle lines have been drawn. Now she's complaining that her dinner was cold and late. Gonna be a long night for this poor man. Oh well...he's from Sudan. If he survived that, he can survive a night with Ma. I guess. I hope. I pray. God bless him.

Nurse is wagging his finger in Ma's face... she's cussing. It's on now.

A nutritionist called Ma's room to take her order for breakfast. After hanging up, the rant went like this:

Ma: Damn people been calling me all day to feed me garbage. This lasagna tastes like dog food. Probably used some of that poison hamburger that's been killing people all over the country. How you think this water is gonna work for me?

--It was a room temperature bottle of Aquafina--

Me: Ma, they gave you a container of milk and some Ritz Bits for your snack. You gonna drink this milk?

Ma: Yeah, if they give me some cereal.

Cell phone rings, see my sister Ginger's name:
Me: Hello.

Ginger shouts: WHAT THE HELL!

Me: Oh, you called Ma at the hospital?

Ginger: Yes.

Ma: LeBron has some big arms at the top. Look at those muscles. Do you think he works out?

Game is less than 5 minutes from the end of the third quarter:

Ma: Who's in the white clothes?

———

I'm in bed and I hear Ma kinda screaming in her sleep. I go downstairs to check on her:

Me: Ma wake up. You okay?

Ma: Yeah.

Me: You were screaming.

Ma: Oh, must've been having a "sleepmare."

———

Me: His name is Buttigieg, not Buttibutt.

———

Me: This banana cream cake is kinda dry.

Ma: Banana cream cake is always kinda dry. So is banana bread. The only thing that's not dry is banana pudding.

Me: Ummm, I don't think any kinda pudding is dry, Ma.

———

Ma: If you've seen one slave story you've seen 'em all... *12 Years a Slave, The Help.*

Me: *The Help* wasn't about slaves. They were maids.

Ma: In the south. Slaves.

———

All of a sudden Ma is going on and on about neckbones and potatoes. Must be hungry.

———

Ma: I only eat the cheese. I don't eat the liquid stuff. What's it called?

Me: Salsa

———

Ma: Well, it's difficult, but somebody's gotta do it.

Me: Do What?

Ma: Go to bed.

———

Ma: I think my blood sugar done dropped sky low.

———

Ma and I are Christmas shopping when she got mad:

Ma...I know your eyes are getting bad, but certainly you can see the difference between a Black and Decker Waffle maker and a George Foreman Grill. I wanna go home.

———

Ma: She was downright ugly...even for a young girl.

Me: What's young have to do with it?

Ma: Well, young girls be kinda cute, even if they're funny looking. Not her.

———

Ma: I think I'm gonna have to get a new foot doctor. He made that shoe and it's all big and congloberant.

Me: Con what?

Ma: Congloberant.

Me: What is congloberant?

Ma: I don't know. I just made it up.

———

Ma: The string beans may have been good if I could chew 'em. Those were white people string beans. Black people don't cook 'em like that. We put ham hocks in 'em and let 'em get done.

Watching TV with Ma when this brother came on the screen:

Ma: Wonder what he is. He's too ugly to be an American.

Me: Ma, there are ugly Americans.

Ma: Not like that. American uglies aren't as ugly as other uglies.

Ma: In Roweeda, where they were killing the children.

Me: Rwanda, Ma.

In November 2010 the Giants won the World Series:

Ma: Wow, the Giants won the World Series for the first time since 1954. Probably don't even have the same players.

Mom joined the "Y" to attend the Silver Sneakers program for senior citizens. Would someone please tell me how in the world a person gets so worn out from CHAIR aerobics?

———

My mother literally devoured Fifty Shades of Gray. With her bad eyes, she's sat down with her magnifying glass and is about to finish that doggone book.

Ma: It's a triology. We need to get the other two.

--Guess now that she's done, I can finally read it.--

———

So, Mom and I bought the two sequels to *Fifty Shades of Gray*. I get up in the middle of the night to use the restroom and saw light shining in the hallway. I walk out of my room and see the light is coming from her room. There she is, sitting on the edge of her bed, book in one hand, magnifying glass in the other...reading. I've created a monster.

———

Okay, whassup with my mother? Ever since she finished reading the *Fifty Shades of Gray* trilogy she's been saying "kinky fuckery." Ohhh, Ma.

———

Me: Ma, you should go the library sometimes. It's right across the street.

Ma: I don't read books anymore unless they have pictures or are magazines.

Me: You read the *Fifty Shades* trilogy.

Ma: That's 'cause it was about sex. I'd never heard of all that kinky stuff...butt plugs and playrooms and people tied down to the bed.

———

Ma: Those people on that TV program look churchified.

———

My mother is tripping, saying I ate her Cheetos.

I haven't eaten ONE Cheeto, let alone the whole bag.

Ma is the only person I know who thinks she can eat something on a daily basis and still have some left. She does the same mess with her cereal. Accuses me of eating it, even though she's eaten a bowl every day until it's gone.

———

Ma: Remind me to never, ever go to Walmart again on the first of the month.

———

A white teenage contestant in a singing competition:

Ma: Her butt sits up on her back like a black girl. "Big old bottly butt...bet she's having sex."

My eyes are dilated like a mug and Ma is steady telling me to take her places. She needs to be telling me to take her home since I CAN'T SEE. She always wants to go to the eye doctor with me...but I end up driving.

Ma put a pie in the oven about 45 minutes ago:

Ma: WE stuck the pie in the oven and never turned it on." *(notice that WE).*

--In my head... No wonder I never smelled any pie baking--

Mom getting on me about going in public without make-up.

Me: Well, if I don't look good without my make-up, maybe I should be mad at you and Daddy.

Ma: That girl will lie in a minute... will lie and say she has a degree because she went to college for two days.

———

Ma watching a singer on TV:

Ohhh ooo... everybody always gotta be trying to do runs. She needs to leave that shit out.

———

Gabrielle Sidibe is on TV:

Ma: God, look at her...that child gonna die.

———

Ma calls my name. I answer. Nothing. Calls again. I answer again:

Ma: I didn't want anything. I think sometimes your name just comes outta my mouth.

--In my head… Boy, don't I know it--

———

I'm reading someone's obituary to Mom and it gives the date "she met her demise":

Ma: Who is demise?

———

Ma: Why is Chris Crispy...

Me: Christie, Ma.

Ma: What did I say?

Me: You said Crispy.

Ma: Oh well.

———

So, last night Mom and I were watching "Bluebloods" (one of her favs). The plot centered around the death of one Hasidic Jewish man and the murder of his son. One character used the phrase 'sitting shiva':

Me: I wonder if he was involved in the murder?

Ma: Isn't he the one named sitting shiva?

Me: *--LAUGHING HYSTERICALLY-- (as I explained what sitting shiva means).*

———

Ma and I are in the car. She's chomping on a bag of potato chips. About 15 minutes in she holds up the bag:

Ma: Want some of these crumbs?

--This chick offered me crumbs.--

———

My mother is turning into quite the little Archie Bunker clone - Jeopardy category - Dance Origins:

Answer - Lambada:

Ma: "Puerto Rico"

Alex Trebek: "Brazil"

Ma: "Well, they're the same."

Me: "No they're not."

Ma: "They all speak Spanish."

On my way home I stopped for take-out Chinese food:

Ma: Where'd you get this food?

Me: Place not too far from the house. First time trying it.

Ma: This pepper steak tastes kinda burned. Not all Chinese people can cook Chinese food. Sometimes I wonder if they're even Chinese. Could be Japanese or Korean.

Me: Not all Asian people look alike.

Ma: They do to me. I'm not Asian.

One morning as the trash was being collected, I heard the truck crunching on the ice. As I got dressed for work Ma came in my room and said, "They got the trash, but it's so slippery out there we probably won't be able to bring the can back." I told her I'd get it. So, I crunched across the icy grass instead of walking down the even more icy driveway. The grass was so icy the wheels on the can rolled on top of it without sinking. It was a bit of a struggle.

I put the can in its place and was about to get in my car and (wait for it, wait for it):

Ma: YOU WENT ALL THE WAY DOWN THERE TO GET THE CAN AND YOU DIDN'T BOTHER TO CHECK THE MAILBOX.

So, I go crunching back across the front yard down to the mailbox...only to report back that it was still empty; we probably didn't get a delivery yesterday because the street was so icy.

--In my head... DOGGONE YOU, MA. You and that damn mail—

Going through the drive-thru:

Ma: You can tell by her voice she's good and Black.

When a person don't want nothin'
that's exactly what they get…nothin'.

Three days post-op from my eye surgery and Ma fusses because I inadvertently bent over. Then she turns right around and asks me when I'm going to bring down the Christmas decorations. How about NOT TODAY.

———

Ma on Kevin Hart: That's the blackest little man.

———

Ma: What's his name...the little black actor?

Me: Kevin Hart

Ma: Yeah. He took a woman shopping at J.C. Penney.

———

Ma: What's a roadie?

Me: The technical crew who travels with the band and sets up all the gear and makes sure everything is working.

Ma: I guess I'm your roadie, huh?

Me: Ma, you've never even put a mic on a stand. You're more of a groupie.

Ma: What's that?

Me: Nevermind.

———

Me: They say Lamar Odom had even taken a bunch of organic Viagra.

Ma: So he could keep going.

———

Ma: Cooch and Kang

--*Translation – Cheech and Chong*--

———

Ma went outside to get the mail:

Ma: I don't know whether that was a lizard or a frog

Me: Where?

Ma: Out there on the walkway.

Me: Did it run?

Ma: No. I ran.

———

God grants miracles. You just gotta give Him a reason to want to.

———

Ma and I talking about The Black Wall Street in Oklahoma:

Ma: They massacrayed hundreds of Black people there.

Me: —lol—Ma, don't say massacrayed.

Ma: What is it?

Me: Massacred.

Ma: Well, the way they did those Black people, it was massacrayed.

Ma: You need a longer neck.

Me: If I put it on my list right now maybe it'll come next month in time for Christmas.

Ma has been getting neuropathy treatments for leg pain three times a week for several months:

Ma: I only have a few more treatments to go. When I'm done, I'm gonna tell them about it.

Ginger: What are you gonna tell them?

Ma: That the shit don't work.

My bro-n-law got some Cubano cologne for Christmas. The bottle is shaped like cigars:

Ma: What is that...a penis

Her thoughts on Obamacare:

Ma: He ought to just let that shit go and start over next year.

Ma: If I don't get some new teeth soon, I'm gonna have to stop eatin'.

I come in the house and Ma is on the phone:

Ma: Why did he stab and cut her? Was he trying to kill her? Huh???

Me: He's gonna crack up when he sees the picture. I just texted it to him.

Ma: You can text a picture?

Me: Yeah...pictures, video.

Ma: But you can't text money?

Me: -- *crickets* --

Ginger and Ma took me for my eye surgery. Gin spent the night so she could take me to my follow up the next morning:

Ginger: I'm gonna sleep on the couch.

Ma: You should sleep upstairs on the futon.

Ginger: Why? The couch is fine.

Ma: You don't wanna sleep on that cold plastic.

Me: How you gonna call my $4000 leather couch plastic?

———

Ma: I'm cold all the time. Maybe I have hydrophobia.

Me: Did you just say hydrophobia?

Ma: Yeah.

Me: Do you mean hypothermia?

Ma: Yeah. I think hydrophobia has something to do with dogs.

--W-T-F (though that isn't what I said)--

———

Ma said the grease in the food at this restaurant covered her lips like lipstick. Gin, Luther and I are dying laughing.

———

Ma: Why do my boobs look like they're down to my waist?

Me: They're almost 82 years old.

Ma: --*side eye*—

———

Mom's response when Ginger tells her she's trying to lose weight:

Ma: Well, how much weight are you trying to lose. I could see you're fat.

———

Mom and I are in the car after going shopping. I had a mix CD playing in the car and Dr. Funkenstein came on. Ma looked at me all crazy:

Me: What's wrong?

Ma: Why are you playing that song? It's so old.

———

Why is Ma mixing up "How to Get Away with Murder" and "Murder She Wrote"…dang.

———

Watching Dancing with the Stars and Ma says this about contestant/rapper Nelly:

Ma: His eyes must be going bad. He keeps wearing those glasses.

———

Ma and I are in the car and an Aretha song comes on:

Me: Did you like Aretha Franklin?

Ma: Yeah, I liked some of her songs, like that one about the yellow car.

Me: Uh, the pink Cadillac?

Ma: -- LOL —pink Cadillac…yellow car…LOL.

———

Ma and I were watching Scandal and something was going on with Quinn:

Ma: Where did they get that dumb ass broad from? Wonder why they don't get rid of that crazy-ass woman.

———

Ma on Scandal character Mellie Grant having been raped by her father-in-law:

Ma: I would've wrung that penis off. Broke it. He wouldn't have put that thing in me.

———

Ma's comments while watching a sex scene on Scandal:

Ma: That Shonda Rhimes....do you think she gets any sex?"

Okay, so why is Ma on the phone explaining the origins of the Crips, Bloods and Black Panthers to my cousin.

Show on t.v. airing old music clips from artists, including Vanilla Ice, who said, "Word to the mutha."

Ma: What does that mean, mother fucker?

Me: Ahhhh. Here we go.

Only two of us in this house right now and I'm the one who DIDN'T take a chunk out of that mac 'n cheese, Ma.

Some folks you have to feed out a long handled spoon.

Well, Ma and I are in the car and the song Have You Ever comes on the radio:

Ma: Who is that? Is that the guy who was discovered by the famous man in Hollywood?

Me: The guy discovered by the famous man. I have no idea who you're talking about. But, no, that's Brandy.

Ma: That's Brandy? She sounds really good.

Me: Ma, Brandy will sing a great singer under every table. She can go.

Ma: I didn't realize she was that good.

Me: Yep. She is.

Ma: Her brother, Ray J, can he sing, too?

Me: No.

Ma: Well, what's he famous for?

Me: Being Brandy's brother.

Ma: Wasn't there something about him and Kim Kardashian?

Me: Yeah. But, he's Brandy's brother. Let's just leave it at that.

Ma: Hey, you're sitting on my hat.

Me: Your hat is on your head.

———

Ma: There are a lot of big butt white women in Richmond. Seems odd seeing white women with great big butts.

———

Ma and I are trying to remember someone's name. We knew his last name, but the first one wasn't coming to us:

Ma: Chucky

Me: Was that his name?

Ma: That's what we called him.

———

Ma: Is that rain?

Me: It's actually sleet

Ma: Hope it doesn't turn into that really big sleet.

Me: You mean hail?

Ma: *--LOLOL—*

———

Ma: Did you sprinkle some tenderizer on the meat?

Me: Yeah, Ma.

Ma: Oh. You're beginning to become a good cook.

--In my head... I'll have you know I've been throwing down for years—

———

Ma watching Judge Judy...a case about a pit bull attacking a shih tzu:

Ma: Who would take a strange shit-bull into their house?

Me: Ma, did you say shit-bull?

Ma: I don't know. What is it?

Me: A pit bull and a shih tzu.

Ma: *--LOLOLOL--* I didn't even realize I said that 'til you said it.

———

News reports on TV giving safety tips about frying turkeys:

Ma: There'll be somebody on fire.

———

Ma talking to her niece on the phone:

Ma: She went with them on one of those yacht things.

Me: A cruise.

Ma: A cruise.

———

Ma: Lyndon. President Lyndon. What was Lyndon's first name?

Me: That WAS his first name. Lyndon Johnson.

Ma: Oh, yeah.

———

Ma attends a virtual birthday party for her 90-year-old friend in Georgia:

Ma: Nobody had on a mask.

Me: Ma, they're all at home. We didn't have on masks either because we're home.

--confused look-- followed by

Ma: Ohhhh, I thought they were all at Kat's and Linda's.

———

Me: Ma, you want mashed sweet potatoes?

Ma: Yuck. Greens and dressing are enough mashed stuff.

My father used to say there are two people you need to watch out for, a talking man and a quiet woman.

Me: Even though the family isn't exchanging gifts, I was gonna sneak and buy you something, Ma. But, I spent so much money getting the rental house back in order I'm kinda broke.

Ma: You ain't got no credit cards?

The grandmother ain't been born yet of a man I would trust.

That Chipotle…now they done started poisoning people on the East Coast.

A sister on Wheel of Fortune only won the consolation prize money:

Ma: Her hair was too greasy. All that grease was cloggin' up her brain.

Every week Ma does the crossword puzzle in *People Magazine*. This time the laughing was epic. She misunderstood and misspelled an answer I gave her, which lead to 'mart' instead of 'tart'. What would make her think a fruit pastry is a 'mart'? Then, the same misspelling ended up leading to 'Noby Dick' instead of 'Moby'.

Little Vic was just four and had learned how to do 'thumbs' up. He smiles at Ma, clenches his little fist with his thumb pointed up:

Little Vic: Thumbs up.

Ma: Finger up. *(flips him the bird)*

Ma: Is that your typewriter?

Me: Laptop.

Ma and I were standing outside in natural light:

Ma: Ohhhh, your hair is so pretty with all that silver. How did you get it so silvery?

Me: I didn't do anything. It looks silver, not gray?

Ma: Yeah, especially the top and sides. You're just like the Norths.

--Like she doesn't have any gray hair—

———

Young woman in full workout gear and headphones, at an intersection, CLEARLY waiting to cross the street:

Ma: You think she's trickin'?

———

She doesn't look bad, just not as good as she thinks she does.

———

Ma: Gazutti.

Me: Baked ziti.

———

During an episode of Scandal:

Ma: A piece of ass and he just blows his world and everybody else's.

On break #2 from cleaning my wood floors. I'd be moving a lot faster if Ma didn't have the furnace set to crematorium.

It's 2018 and Ma is blasting Eartha Kitt on a boombox.

Ma: I'm glad we decided to keep you after you were born.

Me: Well, uh, what else were you and Daddy gonna do with me?

Ma: Well, we could've just left you up there in St. E's Hospital.

--Crickets-- (now I'm wondering if they were really contemplating that)--

---

My mother just asked me to look up something online for her:

Ma: Why don't you just do a Google search like I do when I'm looking or something.

--In my head ... Well, Ma, why don't you just look it up yourself—

———

Ma asked me to get her a 'daughter' Christmas card while I'm at the store. I bought one for daughter and son-in-law. She tells me she already sent Ginger and Luther a card. I'm confused...until she says the card was for me. So, I'm supposed to pick out my own Christmas card from her...and mail it to myself. WOW! Who does that?

———

Three years later, as we're preparing to move to a new city:

Why is Ma talking 'bout how much she's gonna miss this townhouse? Remember when she was calling it the PROJECTS?

———

Me: It's skating rink, Ma, not ring.

Ma: All this time I've been saying ring. Spend your whole life making mistakes, then learn.

———

I watched an episode of Iyanla Fix My Life:

Me: Have you ever heard of a guttersnipe, Ma?

Ma: Oh, yeah. That's a really bad name, like calling a woman a whore.

The Bible ain't never lied; you sow a bad seed, you reap a bad harvest.

Ma: You got any fruit tea?

Ginger: Just green. I always have green.

Ma: That tells me you believe the hype. Like we're about to get some benefits from green tea.

When Ma saw a picture of Rudy Giuliani's hair dye running down his face:

Ma: Poor child *(laughing)*.

Ma: Why in the world do they call it Sweet 16. Sounds more like a teenage girl's stupid party than basketball.

Every night Ma goes to bed not long after the 11 p.m. news comes on. But one particular evening there was this exchange:

Me: Ma, it's after 11.

Ma: SO.

—•—

Ma: Do you think Captain D was a real person? Arthur Treacher was. I used to love Arthur Treacher's fish. Remember how they used to have that vinegar for the fish and chips? Why are you laughing and looking at me like that?

—•—

Ma is on the phone asking someone:

Ma: Did he have the pandemic?

—•—

Ma to Ginger:

Ma: Did y'all go to shipotee? (translation: Chipotle).

—•—

Talkin' 'bout back in the day:

Ma: Yeah, they lived on Todd Street down from Alice Mills' Whorehouse.

—•—

Ma: They had a cemetery in Pittsburgh.

Me: Who?

Ma: The Chinese.

--I've got to stop zoning when she's talking to me. I have no idea what this conversation' is about—

—

Ma: Did we spend all the So-DU-ko movie gift card.

Me: Fandango, and no.

—

Explain to me why my mother is always accusing me of using all her toilet paper. THREE toilets in this house. I hardly ever even step foot in her bathroom, yet the minute her roll is running low, she starts questioning me...LIKE SHE DOESN'T USE TOILET PAPER. Geez...

—

Ma on Tamar Braxton:

Ma: Poor girl has been crazy a while. She'll get normal, but then go back crazy.

—

Me: Ma, you want some shrimp?

Ma: You gonna cook some? Okay.

Me: Yeah, putting them in the oven.

Ma: Did you find the French fries in the freezer?

Me: Oh, you want fries, too?

Ma: Well, what are you gonna eat with the shrimp.

--I didn't say one word about making fries--

———

Ma: trump is right. He did have way more people out there on inauguration day. They're called protesters. Nobody has ever had as many as he did.

———

Mom and I walked past a couple of men and one of them smelled awful:

Me: Someone stinks.

Ma: It's that fat, funky man...smelling like piss and shit.

———

Watching the 2020 election results:

Ma: This same stuff been going on for days. Bunch of bullshit.

———

Live fast, die young,

make a pretty corpse.

Ma just did a 10-minute monologue on how all Black people don't look alike, but all Asians do.

During the civil unrest in the summer of 2020:

Ma: They went from civil war to civilian war.

Ma: These people 'round here are always runnin'. They run to the James River they run to this, they run to that. Always some kinda race. People in Richmond ought to be tired...and skinny.

Me: I don't like spinning my wheels. I like to get things done.

Ma: If you don't then you ain't Black.

Me: What?

Ma: Ain't that what Biden said?

Watching the Kennedy Center Honors:

Ma: They didn't do the Chinese man yet, OKO MOKO.

Me: Yo-Yo Ma, Ma...LOL

Ma: I used to think Lionel Richie looked like a horse, but he's kinda sexy."

Me: He did used to kinda look like a horse.

Ma: A "cute horse"

Me: LMAO... dang, Ma.

———

Ma: You know, I never heard of Sonny Rollins, but he must be old because everybody else they mentioned is dead.

———

Ma: I want to go shopping on Black Friday.

Me: Ya better call your other daughter.

———

So, she looks at me this evening and, out the clear blue sky says:

Ma: You know, you got some big eyes.

Been looking at me all these years...hard to believe she just noticed that.

———

When trump refused to concede:

Ma: Somebody needs to go there and slap that fool…and his followers.

Watching The Haves and the Have Nots and Hannah is singing:

Ma: I'm sick of her singing. She reminds me of a slave, if it wasn't for the lipstick and earrings.

Ma watching Katy Perry:

Ma: This looks like some little kid shit. Why would they put some mess like this on the Super Bowl.

Watching the Oscars:

Ma: Marsha, March, Mersha, Marshmallow.

Me: Mahershala, Ma. Mahershala Ali.

TV One is on and we're watching a Michael Jackson show. He's singing "Billie Jean" and starts moonwalking:

Ma: I used to could do the moonwalk.

I'm cracking up because I think she actually believes she used to do it. Near the end of the program,

Me: Ma, lemme see you moonwalk.

Ma: I SAID USED TO.

She ain't never moonwalked.

In 2011:

Ma: El DeBarge looks like Clark Gable. And, Clark Gable looked good for 1930.

In 2021:

Ma: How old is he (El DeBarge)? He's fine.

Opening one of her Christmas gifts:

Ma: What's in here, some Crown Royal?

Heard mom on the phone talkin' about me:

Me: Ma, why are you telling folks my business.

Ma: Adult children don't tell their business... their mother's do.

--Guess she told me—

Ma and I are gonna fall out about this heat. Furnace on 80 degrees AND she's got the space heater on, too. DANG...

I kissed Ma goodnight. She smiled and OMG if she didn't look like Uncle Menzo. I burst out laughing and told her:

Ma: Well, he was my brother.

Lady with a HUGE butt walks past us:

Ma: That's a whole lot to sit on. Looks like it ought to hurt.

Ma: Did you see cabbage on that menu.

Me: No

Ma: Then they ain't Chinese.

Ma: That girl is cute but her afro would look better is she would pick it and not have all those boogie beads in it.

Me: Boogie beads?

Ma: That's what it's called when you don't pick it.

--In my head...Maybe she means beady beads???—

So, Ma and I were in the car, talking about music:

Ma: PLACIDO BOCELLI

Me: Ma, there's Placido Domingo and there's Andrea Bocelli, not Placido Bocelli.

Trying to convince Ma that Tom Hanks played Forest Gump, not Gomer Pyle.

Ma to Gin: Y'all gonna have a tidal wave party for the super bowl.

Me: Tailgate, Ma. You said tidal wave.

———

Ma: Well, who is Robert?

Me: R. Robert

Ma: Ohhh. All these years I thought they were saying Art Kelly.

———

Me and Ma in a restaurant:

Ma: That man sure is flirting with you. But you are pretty.

Me: Thanks, Ma.

Ma: Well, you're mine and I didn't birth no ugly kids...you just had nappy hair.

———

Ma talking about a fast food restaurant:

Me: It's Zaxby's, Ma...not Xanax

———

Ma: Now I done got something from the AZPECKA asking for money? I've never even heard of the AZPECKA.

Me: Me neither. Let me see that.

Ma: Here, look.

Me: LOLOLOL... Ma, that's the ASPCA.

Me: What is that?

Me: The American Society for the Prevention of Cruelty to Animals.

Ma: Oh. Okay. Throw it in the trash.

Talking on the phone about the Picasso exhibit:

Ma: He was a vulgar old man...all you saw was titties and butts and stuff.

Ma: What's a blunt?

Ma: You ever heard of *To Pimp a Butterfly*?

Caitlyn Jenner is on t.v. My conversation with Ma:

Ma: I thought that was one of the daughters. He does look like a woman. I think he must've got that genderfication.

Me: What?

Ma: I just heard somebody talking about genderfication.

Me: It was me. Yesterday I was explaining gentrification.

Ma: Don't put this on Facebook *--laughing so hard she was crying--*

Me: Oh, it's going on Facebook.

On Gayle King's interview with Lisa Leslie following Kobe Bryant's death:

Ma: That was a stupid question anyway. If his image hadn't been tarnished after all these years, it ain't gonna be now. All she had to do was look at all those people at the Staples Center to see that.

Ma and I are driving through downtown Richmond:

Me: See, that's the Maggie Walker Statue right there.

Ma (looking at a mural nearby): Ohhh, look at that man, he looks like Mohammed X.

Me (laughing uncontrollably): Ma, who is Mohammed X?

Ma (laughing): I don't know. You got me looking at that Grace Walker statue.

Me (laughing): Grace Walker???

Ma (laughing): I'm so hungry I'm dizzy.

The Hippodrome in Richmond, Virginia named a drink after me on their menu:

Ma: Wow, that's wonderful. The only scary thing is all the other entertainers with drinks are dead.

Watching continuing coverage of the Boston Marathon bombing:

Ma: That looks like an awful lot of cops to kill two people. Don't be anywhere near that many on NCIS.

Ma: Rome was built in a day.

Me: The saying is Rome *wasn't* built in a day.

Ma: I said it was.

--and, if Ma said it, it must be so—

———

Dad was in the hospital, post-op and on morphine. He had been battling it out with his nurses all day, even pointing his finger at them like a gun. I arrived and calmed him down. Then the phone rings:

Me: Hello. I just got here.

Dad: Who is that? Who are you talkin' to?

Me: It's Ma.

Dad: Oh. Yeahhh. Get Frances up here. She'll shoot these mother fuckers.

———

Ma: Remember the Lost Boys of Sudan. They walked all the way.

Me: Walked here, Ma???

Ma: No, they walked across Africa...til somebody gave 'em a ride.

———

Ma and I just went to Red Lobster for dinner. An Asian family was sitting a few feet away. They had two little boys. The youngest boy got out of his seat and was kinda walking around near their table:

Ma: Isn't he cute.

Me: Yeah, he looks like he's about two.

Ma: Maybe three 'cause he's kinda tall. You know, they're normal size when they're little; then they don't get any taller...except for that basketball player.

———

A rap song comes on the radio that I'd never heard:

Ma: That sounds like something new by Chingy.

—It was.—

———

Ma to me on the way home from the NYE gig:

Ma: I'm glad I know you. I'm proud of you and all you've accomplished. I'm happy that you're never afraid to walk away from something that's not working out. I know there are times you've been hurt and cried...we all have. But you just keep going. I'm proud.

———

Mom and I were talking last night. She said she has an itchy area on her back. I told her she should go to the dermatologist:

Ma: I have a couple appointments before your surgery. But, I'm not making any more for a while after that. It's just too much.

Me: It's just the dermatologist.

Ma: I know, but I have to go get my "monogram" and everything.

Me: Your what? Do you mean mammogram?

Ma: *—bursts out laughing—*

———

Ma: Your Mommy is tired and breaking down.

Me: _____

———

On Ma's 83rd birthday:

Me: You had a virtual party.

Ma: Yeah! It was crowded.

———

———

On Ma's 84ᵗʰ birthday after we sang Happy Birthday:

Ma: Y'all sounded good. Maybe you can join the church choir.

———

Me: Ma, what do you want for Christmas?

Ma: Ohhh, just another day.

———

67102-V6